What People Do

Acknowledgments

Executive Editor: Diane Sharpe
Supervising Editor: Stephanie Muller
Design Manager: Sharon Golden
Page Design: Simon Balley Design Associates
Photography: Allsport: cover (top right), page 16 (both); Chris Fairclough Colour Library: cover (bottom right, middle bottom), pages 8, 14; NASA: cover (middle top); Redferns: page 20; Wayland Picture Library: page 12 (both); Tim Woodcock: page 22 (top); ZEFA: pages 4, 6-7, 10, 18, 22 (bottom), 24, 26.

ISBN 0-8114-3720-5

What People Do

Hazel Underwood

Illustrated by

Katy Sleight

STECK-VAUGHN
COMPANY
ELEMENTARY • SECONDARY • ADULT • LIBRARY

People do many kinds of jobs.
Some people work at home.

4

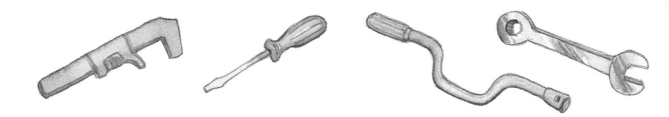

What job would you like
to do?
Would you like to work in
a garage?

8

Would you like to be
a gardener?

Would you like to be
a police officer?

12

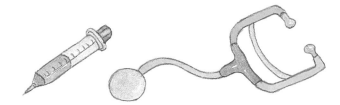

Would you like to
be a doctor?

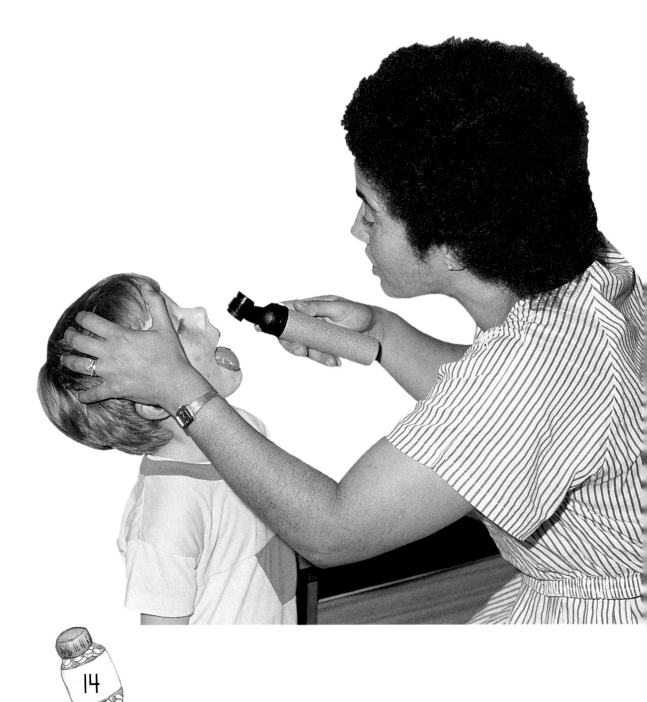

14

Would you like to be a race car driver?

17

Would you like to work in a store?

19

Would you like to be
a music star?

20

21

Would you like to be a farmer?

23

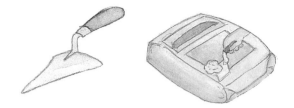  

Would you like to be a builder?

24

Would you like to be a chef?

27

There are hundreds of
different jobs.

Can you tell which
people would need these
tools for their jobs?

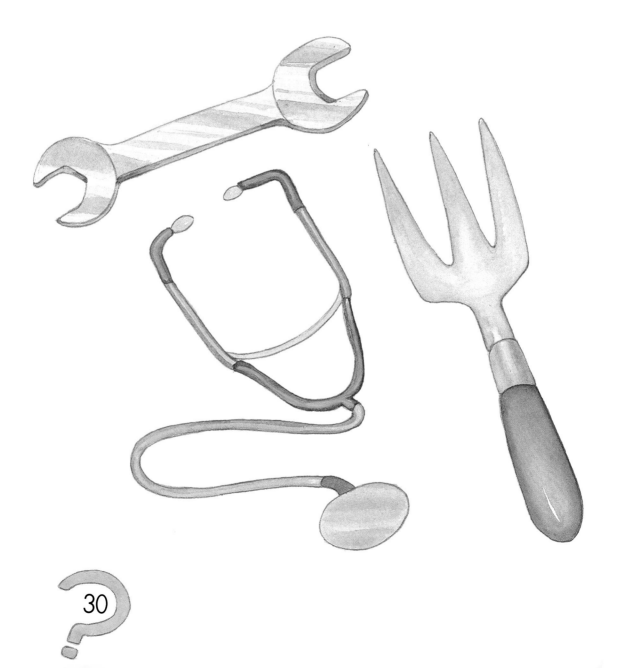

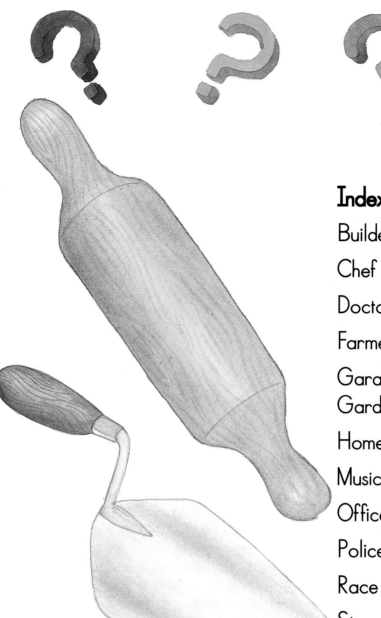

Index

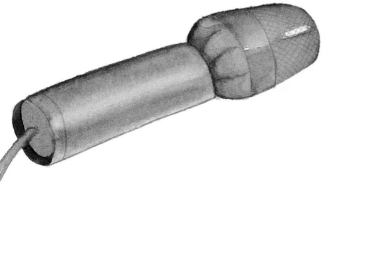